THIS BOOK BELONGS TO:

_ _ _ _ _ _ _ _ _ _ _ _ _ _

Listen! Do you hear it?

A sound like someone sawing logs. A sound coming from a prison. A prison in Philippi.

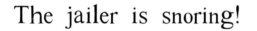

The jailer is snoring!

He's fast asleep. And his prisoners are all safely locked up for the night.

But there's another sound. Do you hear it?

It's coming from the very middle of the prison.
The place from which no one escapes.

And it's coming from two of the prisoners.
Listen closely! Are they moaning and groaning?

They could be.

Their backs are bruised
with the beating they
were given.

Their feet are
locked up in stocks.

But that's not it.
Listen again...

Are they complaining?

They could be. They really shouldn't be there,
you see. They were only helping a slave girl
they met while walking through Philippi.

They were helping her through the power
of Jesus, who died so we can be forgiven,
who came back from the dead so we can live
forever, and who sent his Holy
Spirit so we can follow him
as our King.

But her masters
got angry and
had them thrown
in jail.

Listen once more. Listen closely.
Do you hear it?

That's what they're doing.
Singing songs of praise to God.
And every other prisoner in the
jail is listening to them.

Their names are Paul and Silas, and they
have come to Philippi to tell everyone
there about Jesus, who died so we can be
forgiven, who came back from the dead so
we can live forever, and who sent his Holy
Spirit so we can follow him as our King.

And even though they don't deserve
to be in jail, they trust God, and they
are taking this chance to tell the
other prisoners about him.

Hang on! Do you hear it?
There's another sound...

It's a RUMBLING sound.

A GRUMBLING sound.

A sound from deep beneath the prison.

A sound rising up from the ground.

A sound like a shouting chorus to their songs...

It knocks the doors off their hinges and the locks from off the stocks. And now every prisoner is free!

That's what it is! It shakes the walls and the floors.

But then, listen! Do you hear it?

The sharp scraping sound of
a sword being drawn from its
scabbard. It's the jailer's sword.

He's wide awake now.
And do you hear it?

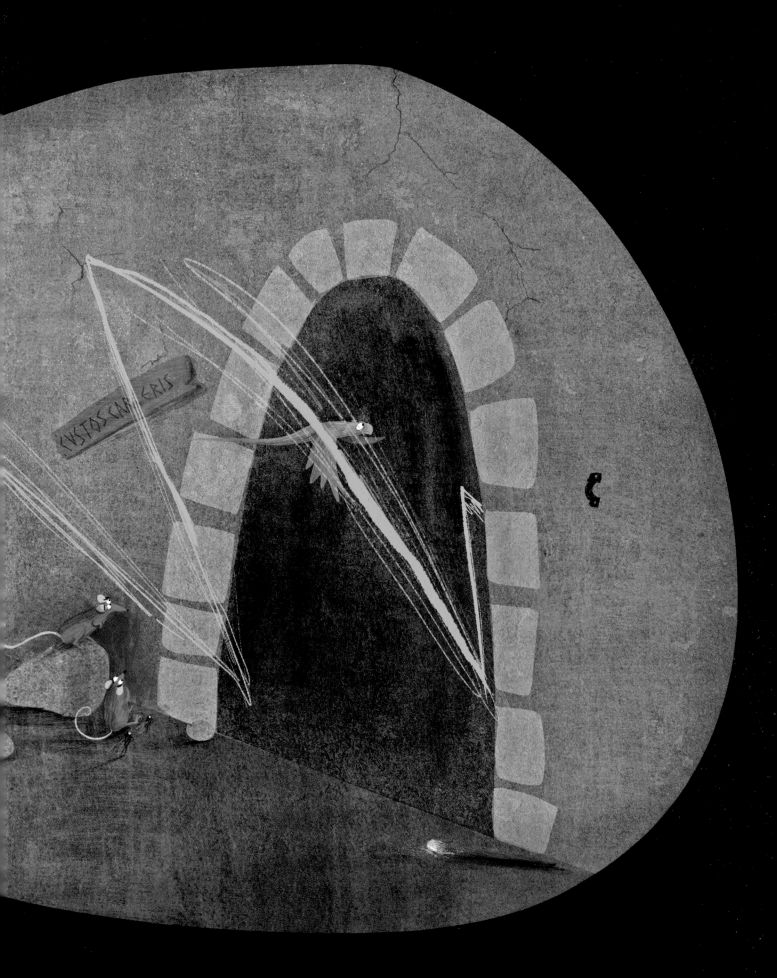

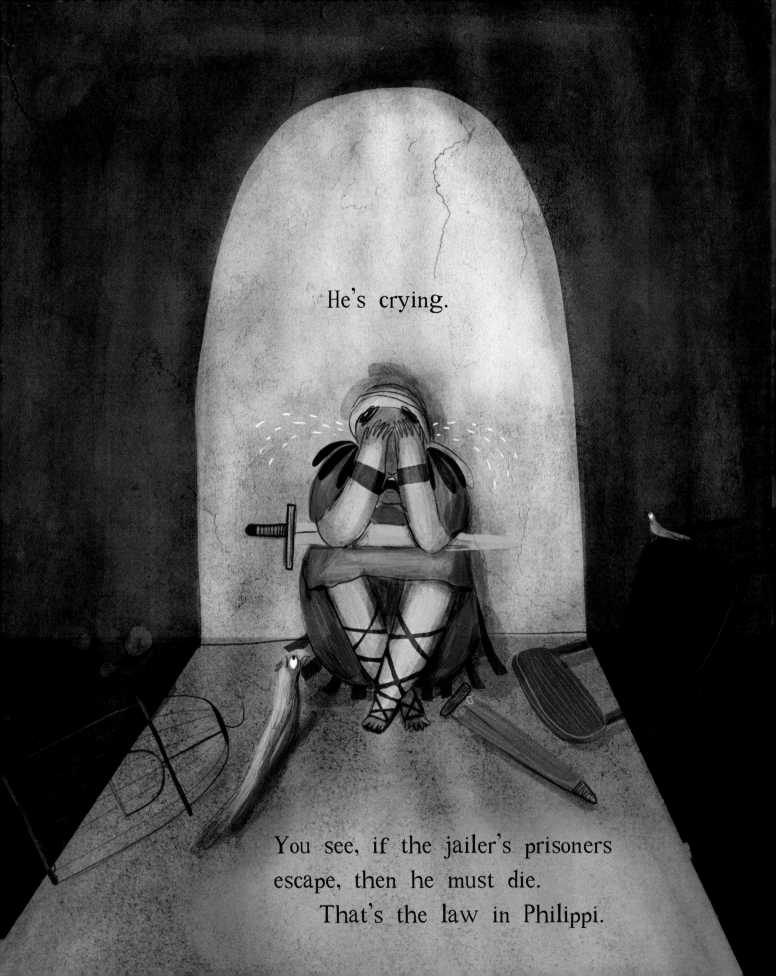

He's crying.

You see, if the jailer's prisoners
escape, then he must die.
That's the law in Philippi.

And when he sees the doors thrown open, he is sure that all his prisoners are gone.
So he takes his sword to take his own life.

And all he can think of is how he will miss his wife and his son and his daughter.

But before he can do that, there is another sound.

Listen! Someone is shouting...

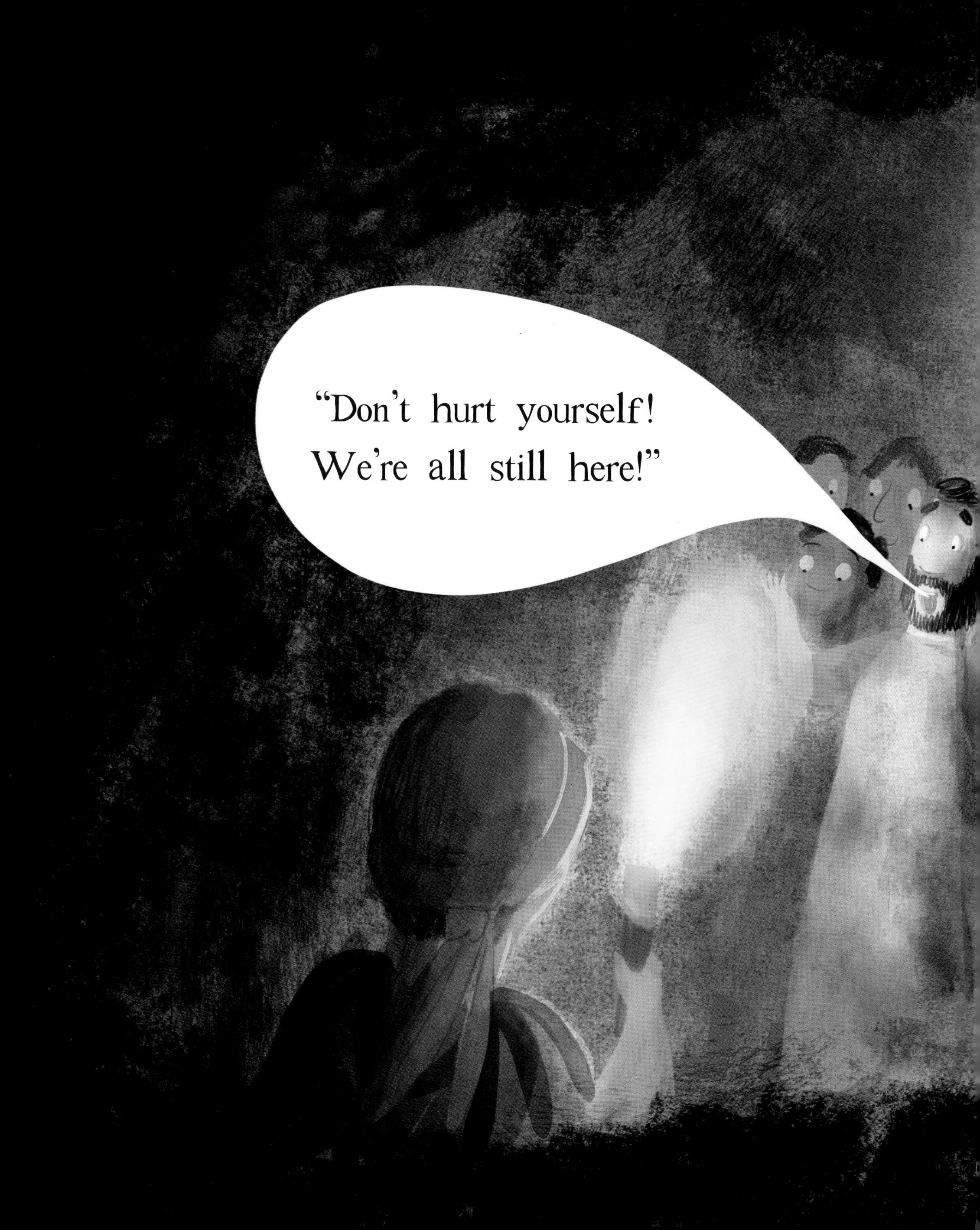
"Don't hurt yourself! We're all still here!"

The jailer can hardly believe it.
So he grabs a torch and picks his
way through the rubble to the middle
of the prison to see for himself.

And when he realizes
that all the prisoners
are indeed still there,
he falls down at the
feet of Paul and Silas.

There is something different,
something special, about these men —
these foreigners who have come to
Philippi with their stories about Jesus.

"Believe in the Lord Jesus. That's how you'll be saved. You and everyone who lives in your house."

Then they tell the jailer all about Jesus, who died so we can be forgiven, who came back from the dead so we can live forever, and who sent his Holy Spirit so we can follow him as our King.

And everyone in his house listens too. His wife, his daughter, his son, and his servants.

And listen! Do you hear it? The splishing? The splashing?

It's water!

The jailer washes Paul's and Silas's wounds.
And then Paul and Silas baptize the jailer
in water, and everyone in his
household too.

Then they all sit down for a tasty meal.

And listen! Do you hear it?

A simple tune.
A set of words...

They're singing!

Not just Paul and Silas but the jailer and everyone else in his house. They're singing and praising God because now they ALL believe in Jesus!

And listen!
Do you hear it?

The sound
of voices.

Millions of voices speaking
in different languages,

all around the world.

In cities
and towns.

In farms and
villages.

In shops
and factories.

And, yes, in
prisons as well.

People telling other
people about Jesus and
how they can be saved.

The same Jesus and
the same Holy Spirit
that Paul and Silas
told the jailer about.

And listen! Do you know
what you can do?

You can tell people
about Jesus too!

HOW DO WE KNOW ABOUT
THE PHILIPPIAN JAILER?

This true story happened in the city of Philippi, in modern Greece. We can read about it in Acts 16 v 16-40 in the New Testament part of the Bible.

Paul and Silas were wrongly arrested, badly beaten, and then thrown into prison. But even so, at midnight they were singing hymns and praising God! Suddenly, God sent an earthquake that set all the prisoners free. The Roman jailer knew that it would be seen as his fault, so he was about to kill himself—but Paul stopped him just in time. "What must I do to be saved?" the jailer asked (v 30). So Paul told him and his family the good news about Jesus, and they all became followers of Jesus.

We see the same thing happening again and again in the book of Acts. Lots of people hear the wonderful message about Jesus and believe in him. You can read about some of them in Acts 2 v 37-41 and Acts 8 v 26-40. Eventually, Jesus' followers began to be called *Christians* (Acts 11 v 26), because they trusted in Jesus *Christ*. Still today, Christians around the world love to tell other people all about Jesus.
And we can do that too.

Enjoy all of the award-winning "Tales That Tell The Truth" series:

www.thegoodbook.com | .co.uk